THE FIRST BOOK OF COLOR

Printed in the United States of America by Polygraphic Co. of America, Inc.

PREPARED AND PRODUCED BY CHANTICLEER PRESS, INC.

Library of Congress Catalog Card Number: 59–5535

The FIRST BOOK of
color

by HERBERT P. PASCHEL

Drawings by Caru Studios

FRANKLIN WATTS, INC.,
575 Lexington Avenue, New York 22

First published in the United States in 1959 by Franklin Watts, Inc.

535.6 —
Pa

OUR STORY BEGINS WITH LIGHT

IF you try to read this book in a room that is completely dark you will not be able to see the colors in the book or even the book itself. But as soon as you turn on a lamp everything becomes visible.

In other words, without light we cannot see. Whether it comes from a lamp, a fire, or the sun, light makes it possible for us to judge how near or far objects are, how large they are, and what colors they have.

So, since we cannot see or judge without light, our story begins with light.

WHAT LIGHT IS

Light is a form of *radiant energy*. Although we cannot see how radiant energy moves, scientists tell us it travels through space with a wavelike motion. We also know that it travels in straight paths called *rays*. Some rays have shorter waves than others. The distance from wave crest to wave crest is called the *wave length*. The number of wave crests that pass a given spot in a given time is called *frequency*.

If we make a chart in which all the rays are arranged according to their wave length, or frequency, we have what the scientist calls an *electromagnetic spectrum*. There are many kinds of electromagnetic rays. Radio and television use some of these rays. Doctors use X-rays and radium rays to fight disease. The ultraviolet rays of the sun can give us a healthy suntan and valuable Vitamin D, but too many of them can cause a painful sunburn. Another set of rays, the infrared rays, is used in electric rotisseries to broil meat.

ULTRAVIOLET	VISIBLE	INFRARED

The Electromagnetic Spectrum

The only differences between all these rays are the length of the waves, the frequency, and what the rays do. As we can see from the spectrum chart, only a limited number of wave lengths stimulate our sense of sight. These visible rays are called light.

WHERE LIGHT COMES FROM

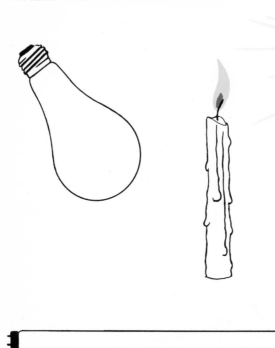

Most of the time we see by the light of the sun. But we also make our own light by means of electricity, candles, fires, and similar devices.

The light that comes from these sources we call *white light* because it does not appear to have any particular color. It appears colorless because it is an almost balanced mixture of all the wave lengths in the visible spectrum. This does not mean that all kinds of white light are the same. Actually they are all slightly different mixtures. We would soon see the difference if we could compare them all side by side at the same time.

LIGHT IS A MIXTURE OF COLORS

When a beam of white light passes through a triangular piece of glass called a prism, the prism bends the various rays at different angles. It bends the rays of shorter wave length at a sharper angle than those of longer wave length. So the white light is separated into rays of different wave lengths. Each different wave length produces in the eye the sensation of a different color. Red, for example, has a longer wave length than blue.

The white light comes out of the prism in a color pattern like a rainbow's. The colors of this pattern are always blue-violet at one end, then blue, blue-green, green, yellow, orange, and finally red at the other end.

If we pass the colors through another prism they will recombine into a beam of colorless white light.

A prism does not create colors or destroy them. All it does is bend each ray of light at a little different angle from that of its neighbor. The first prism merely separated the various rays already in the white light. The second prism mixed them together again. The prism experiment shows us that "white light" is really a mixture of many colors. It also teaches us that the sensation of "color" is due to certain wave lengths of light.

A RAINDROP CAN BE A PRISM, TOO

After a rainstorm the millions of tiny raindrops in the air act like prisms and separate the sunlight into its separate colored parts. The result is the rainbow we sometimes see in the sky after a shower.

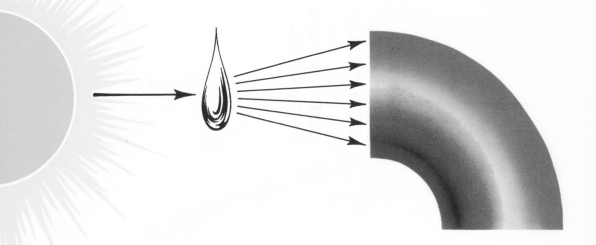

Making Your Own Rainbow

You can make your own rainbow in your garden on a sunny day. Adjust the nozzle of the garden hose so that it will produce a very fine spray. Stand with your back to the sun and with the spray shooting out in front of you. When the spray is in just the right position in relation to the sun, you will see a rainbow in it.

ALL WHITE LIGHT IS NOT ALIKE

A colored object will appear different under various kinds of light. This is so because each type of light has a different mixture of colored rays. The following charts show how much of each colored ray is present in three kinds of white light.

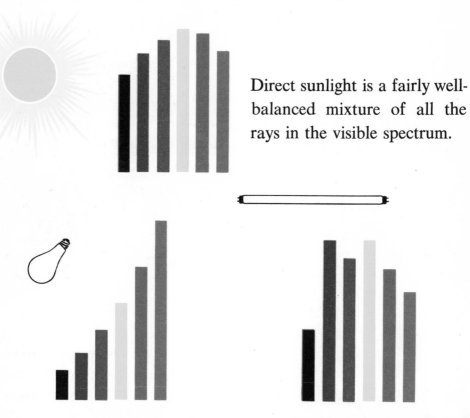

Direct sunlight is a fairly well-balanced mixture of all the rays in the visible spectrum.

Light from an ordinary tungsten filament bulb has many more red rays than blue ones.

The light from a daylight type of fluorescent tube lamp has more blue and yellow than red or violet.

HOW WE SEE OBJECTS

1. Light rays coming from the sun, a candle, or an electric lamp travel through space in all directions. Some of these rays strike the object we are looking at.

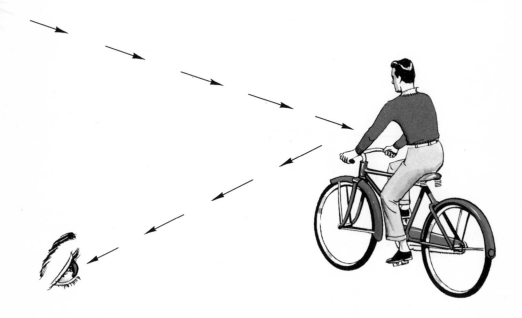

2. Some light rays bounce off the object, and some are either trapped within it or are lost in other ways. Other rays are reflected back toward our eyes. The rays that are reflected by the object are of a different mixture from the original light.

3. Only the light rays that enter our eyes can help us see. These rays excite certain sensitive cells in our eyes and these cells send a message to the brain.

HOW THE EYE SEES COLOR

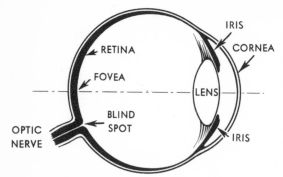

The human eye is very much like a camera. It has a crystalline lens, a light-sensitive layer called the retina, a pupil that regulates the amount of light entering the eye, and an eyelid that acts like a shutter.

In the retina are millions of very small nerve endings that are sensitive to light. There are two kinds: *rods* and *cones,* so called because of their shape. The rods help us to see at night and when there is very little light, but they are not sensitive to color. It is the cones that we depend on for most of our vision. They are not only sensitive to color, but also help us see fine detail.

The color-sensitive cones are believed to be divided into three groups: red sensitive, green sensitive, and blue sensitive. Thus, one group of cones receives the wave lengths of light rays that produce red sensations; another group responds to wave lengths that produce green sensations; and the third group receives the wave lengths of blue sensations. The nerves are stimu-

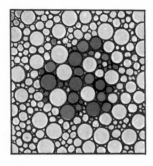

lated by these different wave lengths and flash to the brain the sensations of red, blue, or green. This explanation of how we see color is called the *tri-color theory.* The colors corresponding to cone sensitivity—primary red, primary blue, and primary green—are called the *primary colors of light.*

WHAT MAKES DIFFERENT COLORS

Most of the colors we see are reflected from the surface of opaque (not transparent) objects. Surface color depends upon the *pigments,* or *colorants,* in the surface. When light rays strike an object, some rays are reflected, but others are absorbed, or trapped. This brings about the formation of color by *absorption.*

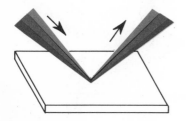

Almost all the rays of white light falling on the white surface are being reflected.

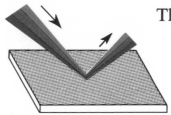

The gray surface is absorbing a little bit of all rays and therefore appears to be darker than the white object.

The black object is absorbing almost all rays. White, gray, and black are colorless, or neutral, sensations. The only difference between them is one of brightness, which is due to the difference in the amount of light reflected.

7/67

WHY A LEAF LOOKS GREEN AND AN APPLE RED

We have seen that light reflected from a white, gray, or black surface differs only in brightness. But light falling on a green leaf or a red apple is changed very much.

Under ordinary daylight a leaf appears green. In the leaf the coloring matter absorbs, or traps, all the light except the green rays. These reflected rays excite our eyes to create a green sensation.

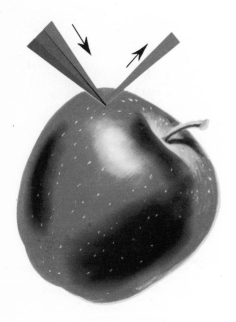

In the case of the red apple, only the red rays remain to be reflected; all other rays are absorbed by the colorant in the apple. When only certain rays are taken from the light by the colorants the process is called *selective absorption*.

COLORED LIGHT

A colored light, such as that from a neon sign in color, will influence the color of an object.

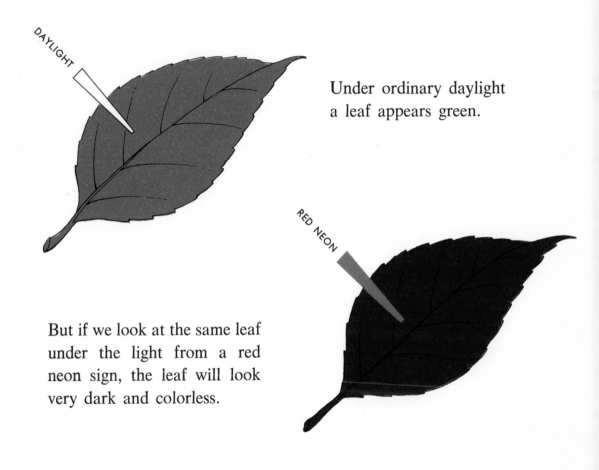

Under ordinary daylight a leaf appears green.

But if we look at the same leaf under the light from a red neon sign, the leaf will look very dark and colorless.

The reason for this is that the red neon light does not contain many rays that the leaf can reflect.

HOW SURFACE TEXTURE AFFECTS COLOR

When light is reflected from a surface, both the texture of the surface and the colorant influence the color we see.

The surfaces of the objects we see range from perfectly smooth (glossy) to very rough (dull).

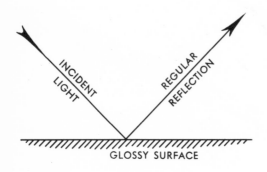

Glossy surfaces act like a mirror, reflecting light mostly in one direction.

Dull surfaces reflect light in many directions, and the rougher the surface the more the light will be scattered.

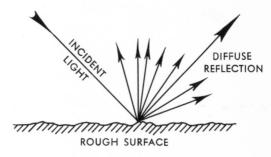

With any surface, a certain amount of light is reflected directly without being changed by the colorant of the object. The light we see, then, is a mixture of the light that is reflected without change and the light that has been affected by the colorant of the surface.

HOW THE POSITION OF THE SUN CHANGES DAYLIGHT

The light from the sun itself never changes, but the mixture of the rays that finally reach the earth does change. The position of the sun (depending on the time of day and the season) and atmospheric conditions (including dust, moisture, and clouds) influence the light that gets through to the earth.

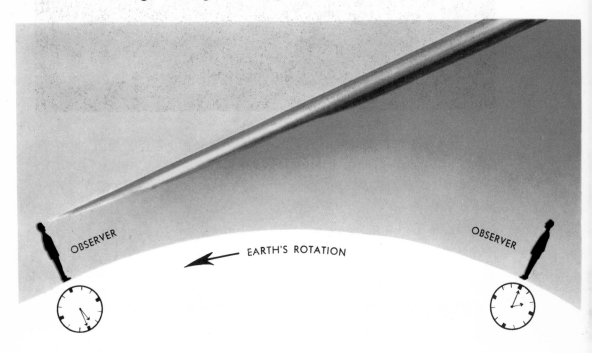

In mid-afternoon, on a clear day, the sky appears a deep blue. This is because dust and moisture in the air scatter and reflect more of the blue rays of sunlight to the earth.

Toward evening the sunset appears orange or red because at that time most rays that get through to us are orange or red. The shorter blue rays are scattered and lost in the atmosphere.

COLOR CHANGES AS DAYLIGHT CHANGES

Everyone knows that daylight changes in appearance throughout the course of the day. This change is due to the difference in the mixture of the colored rays in the sunlight at different times. As daylight changes, color changes. Below is a landscape and hills seen in late morning light. Above is the same scene after sunset.

COURTESY EASTMAN KODAK COMPANY

EVERY COLOR HAS THREE DIFFERENT QUALITIES

We know from our everyday experiences that we have thousands of distinct color sensations. But, surprisingly, these sensations differ only in three ways.

First, there is the difference in the color itself—red, green, blue, yellow, and so on. This is called *hue.*

Second, there is a difference in the brightness of the same colors—as, for example, in red and pink. This is called *brightness* or *value.*

Third, some colors are brilliant and clean, while others seem drab and dirty. This quality is called *saturation* or *purity.*

23

A HUE CIRCLE OR COLOR WHEEL

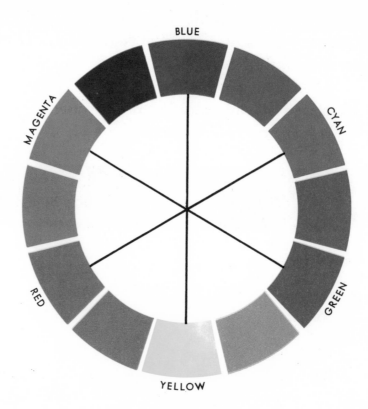

Color wheels, or *hue circles,* show us the relationship between the various colors. They are nothing more than the visible spectrum bent into a circle. The hues are arranged in the same order as they come out of a prism, that is, according to wave length. The one exception to this arrangement is purple and violet, which do not actually appear in the spectrum because they are a mixture of red and blue rays. However, to form the completed circle, they are arranged in the proper order between the blue and red.

COMPLEMENTARY COLORS

As dress designers, decorators, painters and others know, certain colors set each other off and serve especially well for purposes of contrast. This results from the fact that some colors are *complementary* to each other.

Scientifically, complementary colors are based on wave length. Any two surface colors (such as dyes, paints and inks) are said to be complementary if, when mixed, they cancel each other out and produce a neutral sensation such as gray or black.

In the color wheel on the opposite page the complementary colors fall directly opposite each other.

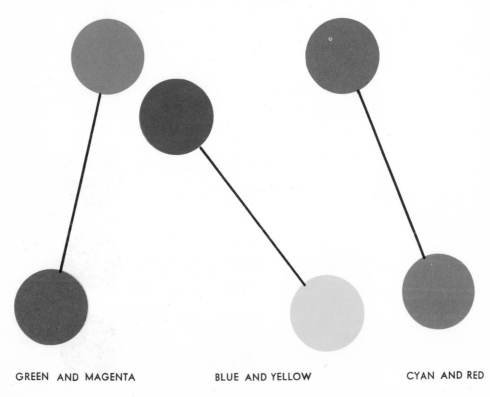

GREEN AND MAGENTA   BLUE AND YELLOW   CYAN AND RED

TINTS, TONES, AND SHADES

The diagram below shows how many different ways a single color can vary.

When we combine a color with white we produce a variation in the brightness of the color. This we call a *tint*.

When we combine a pure color with black we produce a variation in saturation or purity. This we call a *shade*. By mixing a color with its complementary we can also darken it without changing its hue.

When we combine gray (which is a mixture of black and white) with a color we produce a *tone*.

VARIATIONS POSSIBLE WITH A SINGLE COLOR

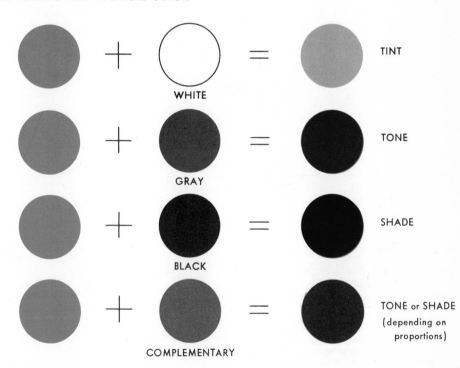

WHITE   TINT

GRAY   TONE

BLACK   SHADE

COMPLEMENTARY   TONE or SHADE (depending on proportions)

MIXING THE PRIMARY COLORS

MAGENTA   YELLOW   CYAN

In surface colorants such as paints, inks, and dyes, the fundamental or *primary* colors are magenta, yellow, and cyan. They are called primary because every other color can be produced by mixing them together in various proportions or by adding white, gray, or black to them.

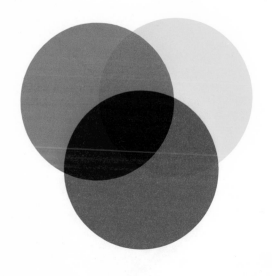

As can be seen from these overlapping circles of color, a mixture of equal parts of magenta and yellow produces red; a mixture of cyan and yellow produces green; and a mixture of cyan and magenta produces blue. The mixture of all three colors in equal parts produces black.

HOW TWO COLORS PRODUCE A THIRD

A surface made up of a mixture of equal parts of magenta and yellow appears red. When white light strikes it, the magenta absorbs green rays from the light, and the yellow absorbs blue rays. Since both the magenta and yellow reflect all the red rays, the surface appears red.

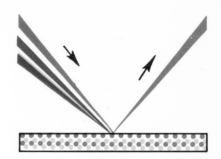

Cyan and yellow produce green because the cyan subtracts the red rays, and the yellow subtracts the blue rays, and both reflect the green rays.

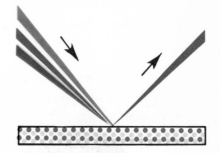

Since magenta absorbs green light, and cyan absorbs red rays, only the blue rays remain to be reflected from this surface.

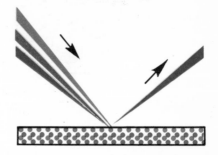

HOW COLOR PRINTING MIXES THE COLORS

In order to print colored pictures on paper, special printing plates must be made. These plates are prepared in such a way that they will take ink only on the areas we want to print. The ink from these areas is then transferred to the paper, usually by being pressed onto the paper. A rubber stamp is a simple example of one type of printing plate.

Four plates are generally used in full color printing—three for the primary colors and one for black. The black plate is added to the three color plates because it restores some of the detail and contrast that is lost in the color plates.

In order to reproduce the various tones of a picture, we use a process in which the tones are transferred to the paper in the form of very small dots. The picture on the printing plate is made up of a great many dots.

Above is a magnified section of a black plate, showing the dots that make it up.

The larger the dots of any one color in a given area, the darker the tone will be in that area. The dots will vary in size in direct relationship to the tones of the original. When the dots become large enough to unite they form a solid tone, as in the magnified view of a color illustration below.

FOUR SEPARATE COLOR PLATES ARE MADE

The picture to be printed must be separated into its four basic colors. This is done by a special kind of photography that separates the original picture into four colors and also creates the necessary dots. Four separate plates are made, each one showing a different color.

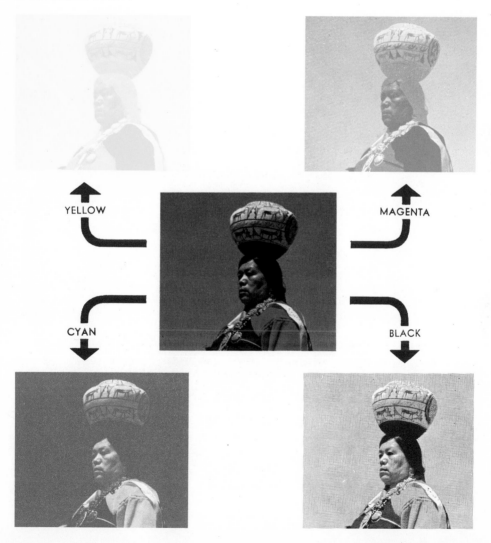

YELLOW

MAGENTA

CYAN

BLACK

PRINTING THE COLORS

The metal printing plates are fixed in position on a large printing press and this press prints each of the four colors, one at a time. We start with white paper that reflects all colors equally.

The yellow plate, printed in yellow ink, will supply yellow to all areas that require it. The white paper, of course, does not carry ink where white areas are needed.

The magenta plate, printed in magenta ink, contributes magenta to the picture.

If the yellow plate is printed first and the magenta on top of it, the result will be some yellow areas, some magenta areas, and some areas combining yellow and magenta to give such in-between colors as red and orange.

The blue-green plate supplies blue-green to the complete picture.

When the blue-green plate is printed on top of the yellow and magenta, the result will be a combination of all three inks. White light reflected from the open spaces between the dots blends with the color to create tints.

Finally, there is the black plate, which adds sharp detail and contrast.

When the black is printed on the three colors, we have the finished four-color picture. When we look at the printed picture, the transparent colored layers of ink control the light reflected to our eyes. We thus receive the same red, green, and blue reflections from the printed picture that we did from corresponding points in the original.

COLOR AND OUR FEELINGS

We often call various colors "warm," or "cold." This does not mean that some colors actually have more or less heat than others. Rather, we speak of colors as we do because some of them (the warm ones) stimulate us, while others (the cold ones) depress us. Our feelings are quite real, but they are not due to any power in the colors themselves. Instead they result from the thoughts and sensations we connect with color.

Although we do not realize it, our feelings about colors depend on our normal experience with them. Thus red and orange generally suggest warmth and heat because they remind us of the hot summer sun and of objects that become "red hot."

We also think of red as hot because we associate it with fire. For the same reason we probably also associate it with danger.

Since red is also a color that attracts attention, we generally use it as a warning or danger signal, in traffic STOP lights, in red flags hung as a warning of danger, and in FIRE EXIT lights. In business, red ink is usually used to indicate debts.

However, when not too much of it is used, red has great appeal. Some tests show that women prefer it to all other colors.

Too Much Blue Depresses

Too much blue seems to have the power to make us feel gloomy. This may or may not be the result of the fact that winter, when the blue colors are seen the most, is a drab season during which people are less active. Some people react so strongly to blue that they describe a mood of depression by the phrase "feeling blue." We call melancholy songs "blues," and we often speak of the first work day or school day in the week as "blue Monday."

But this feeling seems to be true only when there is too much blue. For decoration or in clothing, blue is a very popular color, especially among men.

Green Relaxes

In general, the color green in our surroundings seems to relax us. Probably this is due to the fact that green suggests peaceful meadows, quiet forests, and the restfulness that we feel in the country.

Because of their effect, soft pastel greens are widely used in hospitals, offices and factories.

COLOR PREFERENCES

The studies of psychologists have shown that most individuals of the same sex have, in general, the same favorite choices in colors. These choices have proved to be similar wherever studies and tests have been made.

The order of general color choices in the two sexes follows. As you can see, there is really very little difference in the choices of the sexes. This information is now being used by industry to make the surroundings of people at work as pleasant as possible.

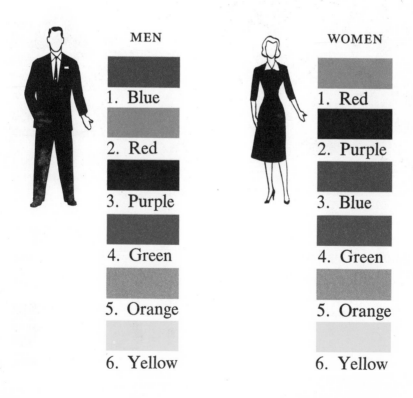

MEN

1. Blue

2. Red

3. Purple

4. Green

5. Orange

6. Yellow

WOMEN

1. Red

2. Purple

3. Blue

4. Green

5. Orange

6. Yellow

COLOR COMBINATIONS AND VISIBILITY

Many tests have been made to find out what combinations of colors are easiest to see. This information is important for everyone whose business it is to get people to look at an object or read print. It is important information to sign painters, artists who make posters or the covers of magazines, designers of clothing or textiles, and others in similar work. It is almost a matter of life or death in making warning signs for motorists. You may have noticed that more and more of these signs are using such combinations as are known to have the greatest visibility: black on yellow, for instance.

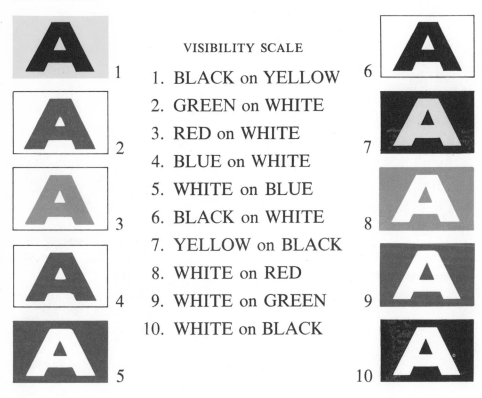

VISIBILITY SCALE

1. BLACK on YELLOW
2. GREEN on WHITE
3. RED on WHITE
4. BLUE on WHITE
5. WHITE on BLUE
6. BLACK on WHITE
7. YELLOW on BLACK
8. WHITE on RED
9. WHITE on GREEN
10. WHITE on BLACK

HOW TONES AND COLORS CAN DECEIVE US

Sometimes our eyes are deceived by arrangements of shades and colors. We may even see things that are not there.

Look at this illustration and very soon you will see gray patches where the white bands cross. But there is nothing on the paper except the black squares.

If you want to see color that isn't there, cut a disk out of white cardboard and rule it off into segments, as shown in the illustration. Then paint each alternate segment with black India ink.

Make a wooden handle—a clothespin will do—and push a thumbtack through the center of the disk and into the handle. Now hold the handle and spin the disk. When the disk is spinning at the proper speed you will see red and green colors.

HOW BACKGROUND INFLUENCES TONES

The tone of an object will look different when it is placed against different backgrounds.

Look at the gray circles in the gray squares. Each circle looks darker than the one below it. But all the circles are exactly the same tone. You can prove it this way: make a mask in a piece of paper by cutting holes in the same position as the circles. Then lay this mask over the illustration. With the same paper background, all the circles will be seen to have the same tone.

This change in appearance always is seen in the same pattern. An object will look darker on a light background, and brighter on a dark background.

The same change in appearance takes place with colors—a red circle will appear darker on a white background and lighter on a black background.

COLOR TONES AND BACKGROUNDS

Neutral tones on colored backgrounds show still another surprising change. The gray arrow in the illustration appears lighter on the blue background than it does on the yellow. In addition, we get the feeling that against the blue background there is a trace of yellow in the gray lines, while on the yellow background the gray arrow takes on a bluish hue.

This strange change always takes place in the same pattern. The *induced color,* that is, the color brought out under the influence of the background, is always the opposite of the background color.

HOW BACKGROUND INFLUENCES PURITY, BRIGHTNESS, AND HUE

Here is another example of the influence of one color on another. If you study the four inner green patches in the illustration on this page, you will surely be convinced that they are all different. You will feel that you see differences in all three of the characteristics of color sensation: hue, brightness, and purity.

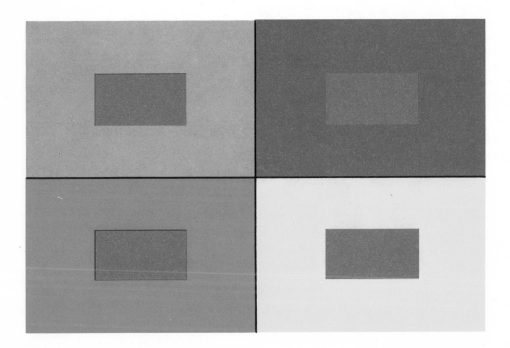

To prove that this difference is an illusion, make a mask that will cover the backgrounds. You will then see that the four inner patches are exactly the same color.

HOW COLOR TIRES OUR EYES

Just as our muscles do, the sensitive receptors in our eyes sometimes become tired. This condition definitely affects our visual impressions.

As an example of what happens when you stare at color too long, look very intently at the black spot in the center of the colored circles for about 30 seconds. Then shift your gaze to the lone black spot to the right. The three colored circles you will then see faintly around the spot to the right are called an *after-image* and are the result of eye weariness, or retinal fatigue.

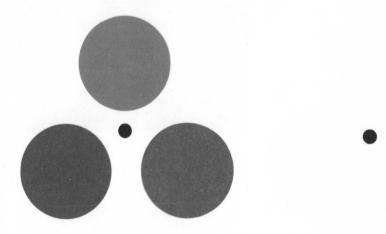

What actually happens here is that as we look at the colors some receptors get more tired than others. When we shift our gaze to the white background, the tired receptors can send only a weak signal to the brain. This weak signal causes the after-image. Moreover, this after-image will almost always be the opposite in color of the original image.

FALSE COLOR IMPRESSIONS

Fatigue of the retina of the eye is often responsible for false color impressions. Especially when we shift our eyes from one colored object to another, the after-image of the first object is likely to mix with our impression of the second.

Stare at the green circle in the illustration above for about 30 seconds. Then shift your gaze to each of the other three colored panels in turn. Against each different background you will see an after-image of the circle, but each will appear to be a different color. In all probability, too, the after-image will be a reddish hue.